Prof. Alfonso de Franciscis
Superintendent of Antiquities in Naples

POMPEII

CIVILIZATION AND ART

Naples Archaeological Museum
Oplontis · Herculaneum · Stabiae

Art Publications
INTERDIPRESS - Via Galileo Ferraris, 132
Tel. 081 - 7349435 - Napoli

© Copyright INTERDIPRESS Naples - Kina Italia - Milan
Text by A. de Franciscis
Lay-out: Studio Matino - Schio
Realization and printing: KINA ITALIA S.p.A. - Milan

POMPEII EXCAVATIONS

HISTORICAL NOTES

The ancient Pompeii lies at the foot of Vesuvius, overlooking the River Sarno valley, not far from the sea. The site is particularly suitable for a human settlement as it is situated on the edge of a fertile agricultural area with good communication possibilities by land or sea. Owing to its position Pompeii was the natural sea landing place for the inland towns such as Nola, Nocera and Acerra and its port was perhaps at the mouth of the Sarno.

In fact Pompeii's prosperity through the centuries was due to its excellent topographic position. However the town did not have its own history and is seldom mentioned by the ancient writers, we must therefore reconstruct events in general terms especially making use of the data furnished by the archaelogical excavations. We know nothing certain of the first human settlements here but as in the Sarno valley evidence of life going back to the Iron Age has been found we can assume that in the IX-VIII century BC in the place where Pompeii was later to be established there was a village or groups of people — the ones who at that time populated the ancient Campania. As Pompeii established itself its contacts with the civilizations prospering in Campania became more frequent and enormously influenced the life of Pompeii. An important Etruscan centre, *Capua*, was in fact not far away overlooking the plain of the River Volturno. Discussions continue as to how much the *Etruscans of Capua* influenced the life and history of Pompeii, but if as some writers say there was an etruscan period of the town, it is here in the oldest urbanistic arrangements, in the architecture and other manifestations of art and life that we find evidence of a continual and prolific contact between the Etruscan world and Pompeii. From the VI century BC the town was also influenced by the neighbourng Greek colonies, especially Cuma, and in fact a Doric style temple was built in the Triangular Forum during this period.

However in the second half of the V century other Italic peoples, the Samnites, spread out from inland and settled in Campania. Pompeii was not spared from this invasion and, although we do not know the exact year, we believe the Samnite community was formed here about 425 BC. The town was later involved in the struggles between Rome and Sannio and in 310 the Pompeians together with the Nocerins repelled an attack from the Roman Navy. At the end of the war Pompeii allied itself to Rome and remained an ally during Hannibal's War.

During the Samnite period Pompeii enjoyed great economic prosperity founded mainly on agriculture, and important urbanistic and artistic developments were made. The defensive system of the walls was fortified and new quarters with wide straight roads and large blocks of buildings were built. Existing public buildings had a facelift and new ones were constructed — the Triangular Forum was adorned with a porch and a colonnade and the doric temple, the theatre and the Odeon were rebuilt. In the centre of the town the civil Forum was surrounded by porches, the Temple of Jupiter and the Basilica erected whilst the Temple of Apollo was rebuilt. It was in this period that the construction began of large, rich, solidly built and nobly decorated atrium style private houses. However the revolt of the Italic allies against Rome involved Pompeii too. In 89 BC when occupied by Lucio Cluenzio's Italic armies, it was besieged by Silla and seized, and in 80 BC it became a Roman colony with the name of "*Colonia Cornelia Veneria Pompeiorum*". With this the history of Pompeii becomes part of Roman history and the town remains peaceful. Only one event in 59 AD is remembered when, because of a brawl between the Pompeians and the Nocerins in the amphitheatre, the Roman Senate decreed a suspension of all performances for 10 years. During this "Roman" period temples and public buildings were rebuilt and improved, among them the temple in honour of Augustus, another in honour of Vespian, the Eumachia building and the large Gymnasium while the amphitheatre dates back to the first years of the town as a Roman colony. The private building industry profited from contacts with Rome and the houses became more beautiful and comfortable and were decorated according to the current fashion. As industry and commerce grew consequently shops and works multiplied. But in 62 AD an earthquake destroyed many towns in Campania and Pompeii also suffered a lot of damage, evidence of which we can see in the buildings that the excavations have brought to light. Reconstruction work was difficult and although private persons' interest encouraged the prompt restoration of the houses and shops, seizing the opportunity to modernize rooms and decorations, the contrary can be said for the public buildings where, work proceeded very slowly and many buildings were still unfinished when in 79 AD Vesuvius erupted.

This cataclysm, which buried Pompeii in a very short time, surprised the Pompeians as well as the inhabitants of other Vesuvian towns which fell victim. The fact is that they had not realised that Vesuvius was a volcano — they considered it to be a green mountain with woods and vineyards. The catastrophe was terrible, and although many people succeeded in escaping, most of them could or would not and were killed by the poisonous gases, by the falling buildings or by the rain of eruptive material. An exact description of the event is handed down by two letters that Pliny the Younger wrote Tacito informing the famous historian about the death of his uncle Pliny the Older who was then chief of the Roman Navy at Misenum. Pliny the Older had seen the eruption from Misenum and had gone to the Vesuvian area both out scientific curiosity and because he wanted to be of help – however when be arrived he too was killed. The archaeological excavations allow us to live

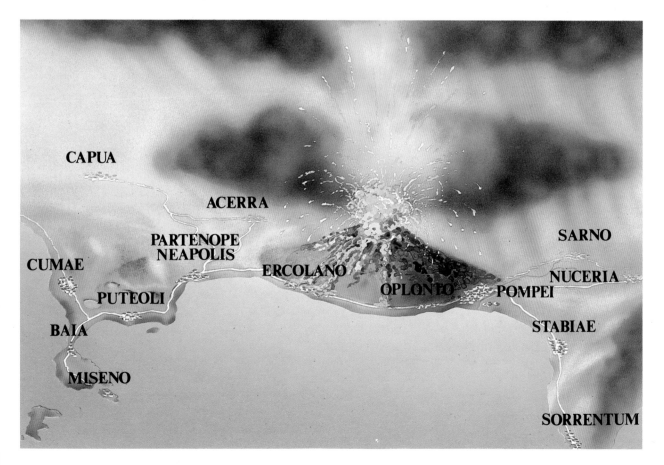

again those terrible moments. With a special method it is possible to reconstruct the Pompeian bodies and from the casts they appear in atrocious attitudes, in the act of escaping, trying to defend themselves from the poisonous gases with their clothes, carrying money or precious objects or seeking safety in flight through the ruins. Pompeii was buried by a blanket of ashes and lapilli more than 6 metres deep and the site was never re-inhabited — only a few survivors or scoundrels returned to rummage and recover. The disaster touched the feelings and imagination of contemporaries and Marziale and Stazio remember it with very sorrowful verses while the Emperor Titus ordered special help for the area. In the middle ages Boethius mentions the disaster and later our humanists from Petrarca to Pontano and Sannazzaro remember it too.

The area was called *the Civita* as long as the memory of the buried

Aerial view of the excavations

TYPICAL PLAN OF THE "DOMUS POMPEIANA"

1) "COMPLUVIUM" - Roof-opening for the lighting up, through which rain fell into the "Impluvium". 2) Upper floor, reachable from a stair beside the hall. 3) "ATRIENSIS" - Housekeeper and entrance-watchman ("Vestibulum" and "Fauces") 4) "CUBICOLA" - Restingrooms. 5) "ALA" - Living-rooms at the sides of the hall. 6) "TRICLINIUM" - Dining-room with three special beds around the table (wall-embedded or movable). 7) "CULINA" - Kitchen; sometimes there was a "Lararium", i. e. a place sacred to home tutelary gods (Lares); service yard; "Apotheca", i. e. cupboard and oven. 8) "BALNEUM" - Bathroom with premises and water at different temperatures ("Frigidarium", "Tepidarium", "Calidarium"). 9) "GYNAECEUM" - Women's quarter. In several houses this quarter, as well as the service-quarter and the guest-quarter, had a separate entrance and hall, which were connected to the cattle-and-carriage-houses. 10) Second "PERISTYLIUM" with a large garden, which was almost always a component of the major houses. Richer than the first one, this garden was adorned with a canal, jets of water and fish ("Euripus"), templets, waterlilies, fountains, gods statues, climbing grapes ("Vitea Tecta") and triclinium for open-air dining. 11) "OECUS" and "DIAETAE" - Living-rooms facing the large garden. There was almost always a side-entrance or service-entrance ("Posticum"). 12) Triclinia (dining-rooms) for the different seasons, or "OECI", "EXEDRAE", as well as other living-rooms and a larger peristylium. 13) "VIRIDARIUM" - Garden with fountains and statues where there was sometimes a kitchen-garden ("Hortus"). 14) "ANDRON" - Lumber-room. 15) "IMPLUVIUM" - Rain-collecting basin situated in the middle of the hall ("Atrium"). At the end of the basin there was a sacred table and an urn near it ("Cartibulum" with "Situla").

town remained but it was only at the end of the 15th century that some traces of the buried town were brought to light and many years were to pass before regular digging was begun. It began, in fact, in 1748 under the aegis of king Charles of Bourbon. Since then the excavation of Pompeii has not stopped and archaeologists study the evidence to gain an insight to the past giving humanity a spiritual patrimony of art and history which is unique.

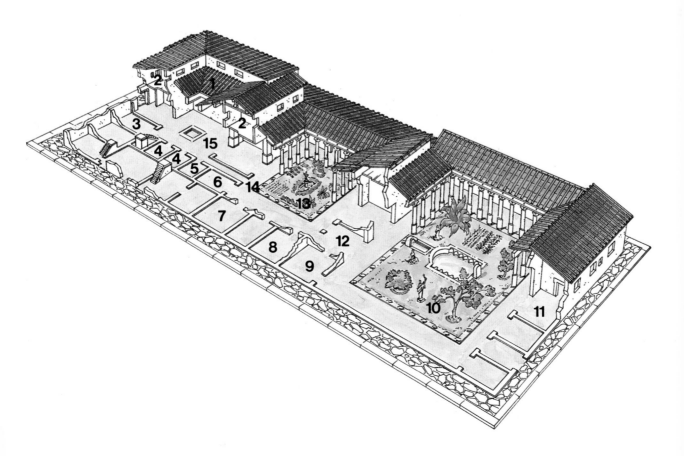

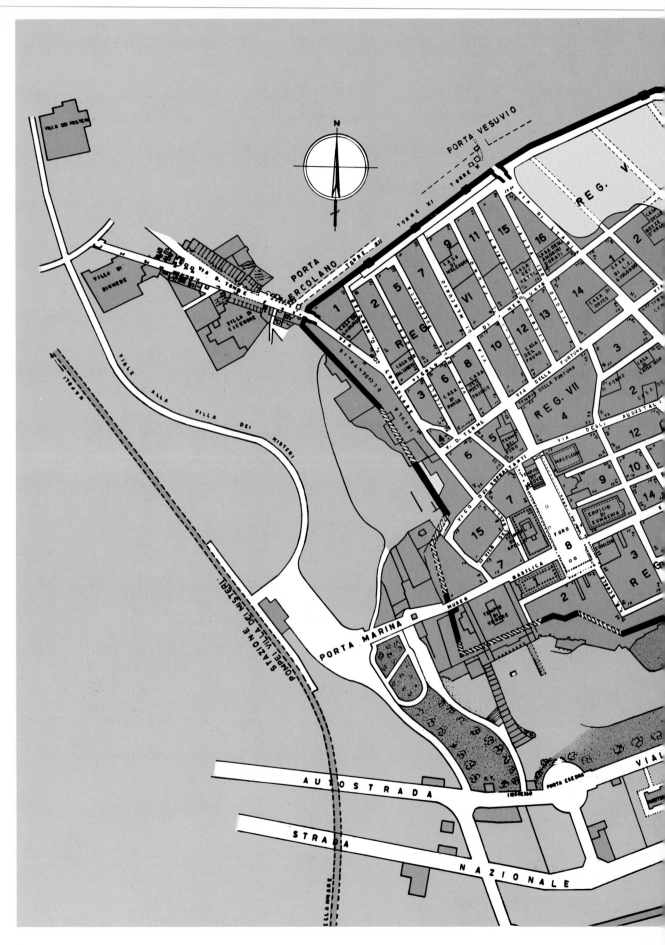

8

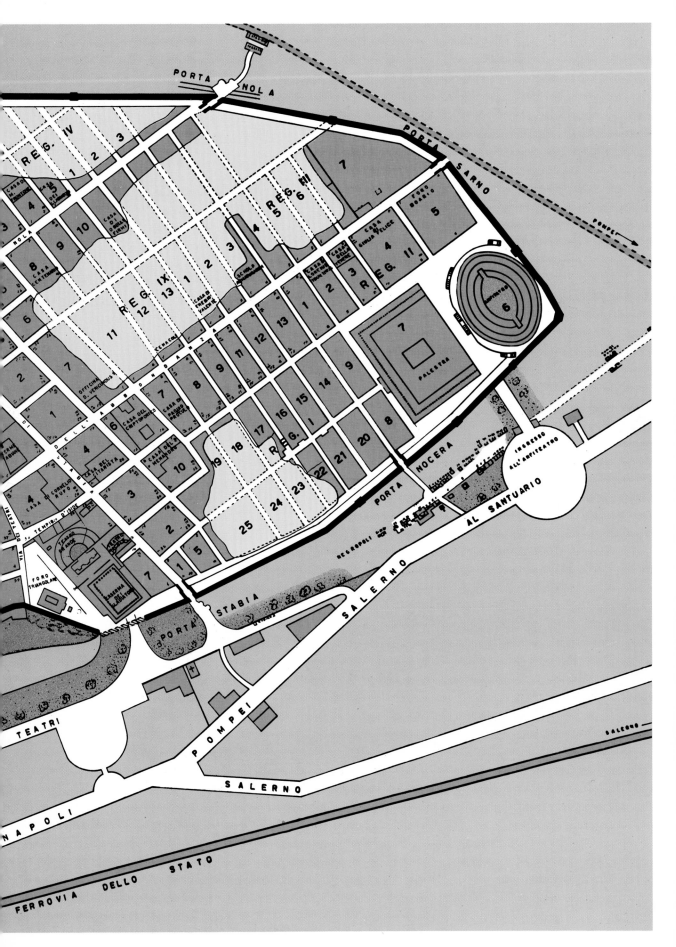

Walls and Gates

The fortifications of Pompeii are well preserved and we can see the entire perimeter and the structural characteristics of same. They were rebuilt many times from the VI to the I century BC but from the appearances which were assumed in the Samnite period we can see a double curtain of square blocks reinforced by pillars and a support to which square cement towers were added in the last construction phase. Only the uppermost parts are missing which must have been crowned with a patrolway and battlements.

In correspondance with the main roads were the gates which have deep passage-ways often divided into two sectors lengthwise. Owing to the preservation Marina Gate, Stabiana Gate, Nolana Gate and Ercolanense Gate give us an exact idea of their original appearance while other gates although interesting were found to be almost entirely destroyed (Vesuvius Gate and Sarno Gate). In fact during the Roman period the walls and gates of Pompeii did not receive any particular care as they were no longer considered necessary during the climate of Roman peace. Many were actually demolished or incorporated into the houses and villas which were built on the town's edge. For the same reason, the damage caused by the earthquake to the gates was never repaired.

▶
The Marina Gate

Roads

Pompeii gives us singular proof of the appearance of Roman roads and shows with what accuracy they were constructed. The roads are paved with a typical pavement of poligonal blocks of various shapes and sizes whilst a different method was used for paving large open areas. The Triangular Forum and the area between the amphitheatre and the Gymnasium are not paved but in the Civil Forum square the pavement which was renewed more than once is made up of large square slabs. It is also noteworthy that here and there stone blocks were placed transversally to obstruct passage at that point. Characteristic also is the frequent presence of large cut stones crossing the road from one side to another — these allowed pedestrians to cross the road without getting wet when rainwater flooded the road — between each stone is a narrow space allowing the wheels of the vehicles to pass. In fact Pompeii had a very limited sewerage system which was not sufficient to drain all the waste and rain-water. Evidence of the intense traffic in the town is given by the tracks, sometimes very deep, that the frequent passage of vehicles has cut into the road paving. The roads were usually bordered by pavements which varied in breadth and in type of paving. In front of the richest houses the paving was particularly well cared for, often with broken pottery mosaics. At many points on the edge of the pavement are holes where wooden poles were inserted to support curtains or tents put up in front of the houses or shops.

Street and Fountain

Typical Structure of Pompeian Roads

Road with Sewerage

The Abundance Street

The Abundance Street - Oriental part

Aerial view of the excavations

The Augustali Way and the Fountain

The Civil Forum

The centre of public life in Pompeii was the Forum, a large rectangular square stretching from north to south, with porches of different ages and styles on three sides and all surrounded by public buildings. Here the Pompeians met for religious and political functions; to strike bargains or just to dally away their free time. A quick look at the buildings in the Forum shows us just how complex and animated daily life must have been. At the end of the square is the temple of Jupiter (father of gods and men) the most important worship place, here Juno and Minerva were also worshipped thus forming the traditional triad of Roman religion. The temple was built in the Samnite age during the second century BC and was later transformed by the Romans into the *Capitolium* of Pompeii. It is an Italic style temple, on a high podium the cell is preceded by a deep pronaos with a sacrifice altar in front. On each side of the temple are two arches erected in honour of members of the imperial family but we cannot identify them with any certainty.

On the western side of the square are the public barns, the municipal treasury seat, the place where measures were controlled (*mensa ponderaria*) and finally the side of the sacred area where the temple of Apollo is situated. This is a place of worship going back at least to the VI century BC but nowadays we see it as it appeared in the Samnite age with restorations made during the Roman period. To the south of the Forum are the public administration buildings, the seat of the duoviri, the most important magistrates in the town, that of master builders and the Senate house where the town Council assembled. Not far away stands the *Comitium*, an area used for elections. On the eastern side of the square is a building built at the expense of the priestess Eumachia — this was the seat of one of the most prosperous guilds in Pompeii, the *fullones'* who were manufacturers of woollen cloth. Then there is a small temple dedicated, it seems, to the emperor Vespasian and a small temple in honour of Public Lares. Next door is the *Macellum*, a large market with shops and also a shrine devoted to imperial worship.

In the neighbourhood of the square are other public buildings, the temple of *Fortuna Augusta*, devoted to a religious cult characteristic of the Roman imperial world, as well as the Forum thermae and the Basilica.

Reconstruction of the Civil Forum

Panoramic View

The Plan of the Imperial Forum

A The Temple of Jupiter
B The Temple of Apollo
C Ponderaria Table
D Honorary Arches
E The Temple of Lares
F The Temple of Vespasian

G The Building of Eumachia
H Comitium
I Duumviri's Office
L Senate-House
M Aediles' Office

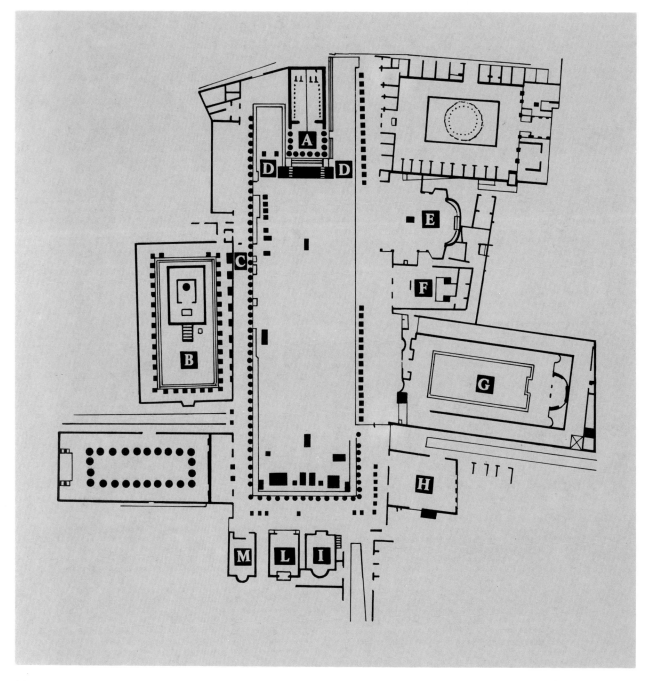

The Forum Street and The Arch of Caligula

The Civil Forum - Western Ambulacrum

The Temple of the Fortuna Augusta

The Civil Forum

The Forum and Vesuvius

The Jupiter Temple

The Civil Forum seen from the Basilica

Airview of the Forum

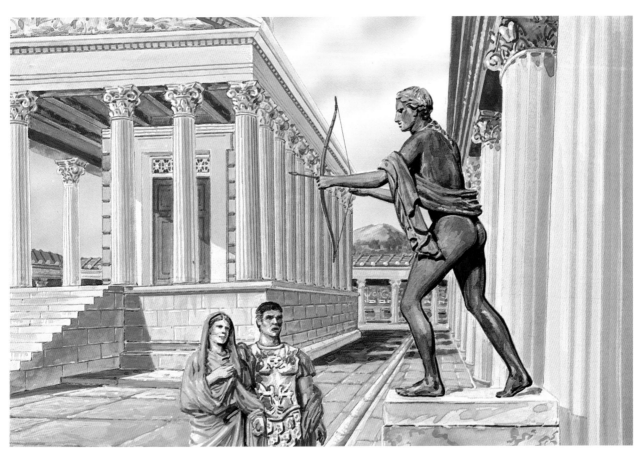

Reconstruction of the Temple of Apollo

The Temple of Apollo - Detail

The Basilica

The Basilica stands at the southwest end of the Forum, the main entrance is preceded by a vestibule, the *chalcidicum*, while there are other two entrance doors at the sides. Inside there is a brick colonnade at the end of which stands the tribunal, a high podium with double superimposed columns crowned by a fronton. The building, the walls of which are decorated in the first Pompeian style, dates back to the last years of the second century BC but the earthquake in 62 AD destroyed it and it was never rebuilt. Many scholars think the Basilica was once covered with a double sloping roof but it is more probable that the internal colonnade formed a continuous porch which surrounded an open central area. Here judgements were made, bankers, merchants and businessmen met to discuss business and like the Forum square this was one of the busiest places in Pompeii.

The Basilica

The Temple of Isis

The worship of Isis originally introduced from Egypt was common in Pompeii. This divinity's sanctuary stands near the Triangular Forum with a high wall and simple entrance determining the sacred area where the religious cerimonies took place. The little temple stands on a high podium and the sacred object of the Isis cult were kept in the cell, the altar is near the flight of stairs. In the south-east corner of the sacred area is a small room leading to an underground cavity where the water of the Nile was kept and on the other side in another covered area the ashes and remains of the sacrifices were gathered. Behind the temple is a large room which was used as a meeting place for the worshippers, the number of which was considerable in Pompeii. We do not know when this religious cult was introduced in Pompeii but the sanctuary as we see it was rebuilt by Numerio Popidio Celsino after the earthquake in 62 AD.

The Temple of Isis

The Triangular Forum

The large square which we usually call the triangular forum has gathered around it other monuments of Pompeii — for example the two theatres and the Samnite gymnasium and in the middle are the remains of a doric temple. This temple goes back to the VI century BC and shows the contact Pompeii had at this time with the Greek towns in Southern Italy and in particular Cuma. The temple was restored in the IV-III century BC but later it was probably neglected and in the Roman age it had become a simple chapel. We do not know the gods to which it was dedicated but during the last period Hercules and Minerva were worshipped here. On the whole the Triangular Forum shows a noble architecture of the Samnite age with a high colonnaded vestibule and a doric arcade surrounding the square.

▼ **Triangular Forum,**
Vestibule

Aerial view of the excavations

Thermae

Three important thermal establishments stand at the cross-roads of the most important thoroughfares in Pompeii, they are the "Stabiane" thermae, the "Forum" thermae and the "Central" thermae. The oldest is the Stabiane thermae which was built in the Samnite age but later enlarged and radically renewed to meet the new hygenic and social requirements of the Romans. The old nucleus consisted of a large communal room and a row of smaller rooms each with a basin and a brazier. The later complex includes a large yard surrounded by arcades which was used as a Gymnasium, and the thermal places were divided, as was the rule at that time, into male and female areas. Each thermal area was traditionally divided into: dressing rooms (*apodyterium*), *frigidarium*, *tepidarium* and *calidarium*. Heat circulated through the empty spaces under the floor which was supported on brick columns (suspensurae) and in the hollow spaces between the walls. The heat was produced in the

▼ **The Central Courtyard**

30

Forum Tepidarium Thermae

furnace which was situated between the male and female sections, the water being boiled in cylindrical boilers. On the other side of the courtyard is an open air pool and rooms used as dressing rooms and restrooms for the athletes. The Stabiane thermae were severely damaged by the earthquake in 62 AD and most of the painted decorations were lost, however most of the plaster decorations dating back to the last years of Pompeii remain. The Forum thermae is a reproduction in a smaller scale of the Stabiane thermae but the decoration is more refined. After the earthquake a new thermal establishment – the Central thermae – was begun but never finished. All in bricks the building shows that it would have been a new architectural conception with wide areas and large windows for light and air and a single thermal area without divisions for male and female bathing.

Pompeii already had a building for theatrical performances in about the V century BC — it was a simple structure which made use of the natural land slope as the Greeks did and had a wooden stage. Over the centuries it was renewed many times, in the Samnite age tufa seats for the spectators were built and in the Roman age the flight of steps was enlarged and the stage rebuilt in stone with an articulated scenic front like the theatres in the larger towns in Italy and Asia Minor. Many of these adjustments were made thanks to the generosity of famous Pompeian citizens such as M. Antonio Primo, M. Olconio Rufo and M. Olconio Celere.

We now see the theatre as it was after the last restoration in the Augustan age. The *cavea* with seats for the spectators is partially supported by a covered passage and to the sides are the *tribunalia* for the more important spectators. The orchestra pit which was no longer used for player's action was occupied by spectators as well. The stage is composed of a low stage where the actors recited and stately background with nooks, aediculas and three doors opening like the front of a palace, columns, tympanum and statues all helped to make the scene more attractive.

The theatre could hold about 5000 spectators. Behind the stage was a square porched area where spectators stopped or sought shelter when the weather was bad.

The Odeon stands near the theatre, it is a similar structure but much smaller and was used for artistic performances which attracted a smaller public, such as musical auditions, recitation of lines and miming and in fact could hold less than 1000 people. It was rebuilt about 80 BC thanks to the generosity of C. Quinzio Valgo and M. Porcio and after this was never again renewed. The flight of steps has been very well preserved and remains a noble example of the late Hellenistic taste flourishing in Pompeii and in other areas during the last two centuries BC. The tufa telamones decorating the end of the *cavea* are interesting examples of the sculpture of this period.

At the same time and thanks once again to the generosity of C. Quinzio Valgo and M. Porcio the amphitheatre was built which could hold 20,000 spectators and this is the oldest Roman amphitheatre which we know. The building is partially enclosed by land but it has no cellars and the entrances to the flight of steps

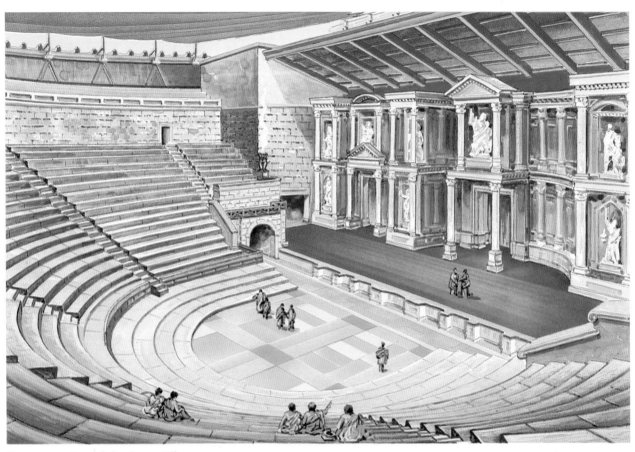

Reconstruction of the Large Theatre

Large Theatre

Odeon - Detail

Odeon - The Telamon

have outer steps. Here we do not find the complicated structure which characterizes the amphitheatres of the first imperial Roman period.

Near the amphitheatre there is a large Gymnasium surrounded by porches and a swimming pool in the centre — here gladiators trained as the many graffiti testify.

The Large Theatre - The Odeon - The Gymnasium   Large Gymnasium

The Amphitheatre

The Houses and Villas

The excavation of a town like Pompeii offers us a large and varied assortment of private houses. The commonest type is the "atrium" house, characteristic of the Italic-Roman milieu. The central nucleus is formed by a large atrium with a roof open in the centre (*compluvium*) and a basin to gather the rain-water (*impluvium*). Around the atrium the rooms (*cubicula*) are situated and at the end, facing the entrance (*fauces*), there is the *tablinium* and behind this a green area — an orchard or garden (*hortus*) opens. As the house has almost no windows on the outside it appears completely closed from the outside. This type of house which may be small and modest or large and rich received in the second century BC the influence of the Greek Hellenistic type house and replaced the *hortus* with a large peristyle which was a garden enclosed by porches and rooms. Thus it can be seen that the principal nucleus with its various parts, the triclinium, hall and bedrooms is transferred to this part of the house. Those rooms along the road which were not used for dwelling opened onto the road as shops or workshops. Many houses, especially the richer ones, also had an upper storey used for other dwellings and rooms for the servants. The rooms had floors with decorations which ranged from simple broken earthenware pieces to mosaic work and of course the walls were decorated with murals which have become famous during the excavation of Pompeii. On the outskirts of the town and outside the walls we can see another type of house — the villa. Here the arrangement of the rooms varies and usually depends on the conditions of the soil and the desire to have large gardens and a panoramic view. The atrium is often smaller but the rear part received more attention ad in fact opens out to become part of the countryside. In these villas, more so than in the houses, we find bathing facilities and areas reserved for agricultural activities, stables, cellars etc. The *suburban* villas and farms scattered on the outskirt of the town are larger and more varied.

The Vettis' House

This house belonged to a family of rich merchants and reflects the tenor of life of the wealthy class of Pompeii in the first century AD. In the atrium are two safes and all around are rooms decorated with pictures of mythological subjects in the IV Pompeian style. The house has no tablinum but the peristyle receives more attention. Here the garden has been reconstructed with elements furnished by the excavations and plants and fountains, so it appears as it must have looked originally. The rooms which open out here are decorated with fine murals and the tricliniar room is one of the most refined examples of Pompeian decoration — the walls have a red background split up by banded pillars and all around runs a frieze depicting amoretti in everyday activities such as the selling of oil, biga racing, goldsmiths at work, gathering grapes, the wine market etc. The servants quarter with an upper storey is concentrated around a secondary atrium and there is also a flat with a porch reserved for the women.

▶
The Vettis' House - Atrium

**The Vettis' House
Peristylium (detail)**

38

A decoration with Cupids

▶▶

▶

The Vintners Amoretti

The House of the Vettii - A fresco

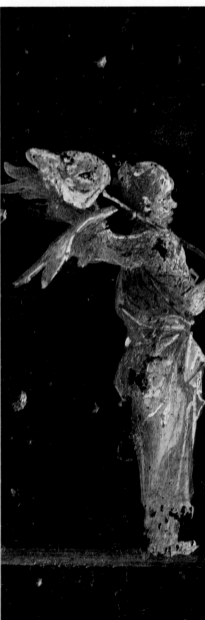

Goldsmith-Cupids

Goldsmith-Cupids (a detail)

42

The Pansa's House

When it was first built in the Samnite age this house occupied the whole block and belonged to one family, probably the *Arriana Polliana* family. It was later divided into more than one house and is therefore interesting evidence of the development of the private building industry which we can note in Pompeii by the middle of the first century AD. At that time prevailing agricultural economy with important landowners was almost replaced by a commercial and industrial economy which changed the social structure of the town.

Of the primitive nucleus of this house only the large atrium and peristyle in the centre of which is a large basin remain. Behind this block is the *hortus* and in fact the excavations have revealed traces of ancient cultivation. In this house has also been found proof that a christian community gathered there in the first years of the diffusion of this new religion in Italy.

The Pansa's House - Peristylium

The House of the Faun

This house, as we see it now, is a remarkable example of private architecture of the Samnite period and dates back to the second century BC but the original foundations go back as far as the fifth century BC. The architecture is noble and harmonious and recalls Hellenistic taste while the wall decoration is moderate and refined in the first Pompeian style with bright plaster squares imitating marble plates. The rooms have mosaic floors which are amongst the best we know, the most famous being the mosaic depicting a battle between Alexander the Great and Darius the Persian King. We can consider these mosaics although not Hellenistic orinals very good reproductions. The house takes its name from the little statue of the Faun in the impluvium which is a Greek original of the third-second century BC and probably belonged to the *Cassia Family*.

The House of the Faun - A detail

44

Reconstruction of the House of the Faun

The House of the Faun - Atrium

The House of the Golden Amoretti

This house belonged to the Poppei family which was one of the most important in Pompeii and related to the Emperor Nero. The plant and decoration of the house testify to a particularly good artistic taste — the atrium is of the Tuscan type but the most interesting part is the peristyle. As usual rooms for everyday activities are situated all around but one side is slightly elevated and appears to be the stage of a theatre with three entrances. We therefore think that this family cultivated dramatic art and here plays for a small selected audience were performed. There is also a chapel in honour of Isis, singular but not unique evidence of private worship to an Egyptian divinity in Pompeii.

The House of the Golden Amoretti - Peristylium

The Tragic Poet's House

This is a small but tasteful house. It is a characteristic house of the Pompeian middle class which passed through a fortunate period during the last years of Pompeii. It is also one of the most famous houses of Pompeii and very dear to Roman age literature. Here can be found two famous mosaics, the first decorating the entrance represents a dog tied with a chain and has an inscription *"Cave canem"* and the second in the tablinum shows a group of players preparing for a performance. There are also fine mythological paintings showing the deserted Arianna, Arianna and Teseo, Venus, Narcissus and finally a picture of Iphigenia's sacrifice which has excited scholars who see it as a derivation of a famous painting of Timante who was a famous Greek painter of the fifth and fourth century BC. This house also had an upper storey of which many traces have been found during the excavation.

Entrance Mosaic (a detail)

The Lucretius Frontone's House

The main point of interest in M. L. Frontone's house is its wall decoration which is extremely well preserved and constitutes an excellent example of Pompeian painting going back to the first imperial age. Other mythological paintings decorating the rooms are justly famous, for example Bacchus' triumphal retinue, Narcissus at the spring, Teseo and Arianna and Orestes in Delphi. The house belonged to well-to-do people as we note from the decorations and the variety of rooms surrounding the atrium and in the rear around the garden is a summer triclinium. On the wall at the end of the garden is a large painting showing animals and trees in an African landscape.

The House of Lucretius - Pediment

The Ceis' House

This house (the owner was L. Ceio Secondo) from its simple design evident especially in the four columned atrium and the decorations in the old Pompeian style goes back to the pre-roman age but underwent radical changes in later times. In fact an upper storey was added which was reached by a stairway leaving from the atrium and divided by a gallery. This newer construction was carried out in a rustic style with a simple frame and is an interesting example of building transformation in private houses in Pompeii. In the atrium there was a wooden wardrobe, tracing of which has been obtained with the special method used in the excavations in Pompeii. At the end of the house is a small garden the walls of which are decorated with a large painting of a landscape with animals and trees.

The House of the Ceis - A fresco

The Menander's House

This is one of the finest Pompeian houses with noble architectural proportions and a detailed plan. Another branch of the Poppei family which we have already met in the house of the Golden Amoretti, lived here. The facade facing on to the road is adorned with two tufa pillars with Corinthian capitals. The atrium is in the Tuscan style and the walls are decorated in the last Pompeian style. In one corner is a little chapel for the worship of the domestic gods. Many rooms open out onto the atrium and one of them is decorated with little pictures of episodes from the "Iliad" – Laocoön, the Trojan horse and Cassandra. Gathered around the peristyle which is at the rear are still more rooms. From one side we can see a large triclinium where the excavations have been carried out in layers showing the first construction phase of the house with wall decorations of the first style. In a small room nearby skeletons of the victims of the eruption have been found. Next come the servants quarters where the slaves lived and then the rustic lodgings and a small courtyard with a stable. At the end of the peristyle we can see paintings of theatrical subjects including a portrait of the poet Menander and from this the house gets its name. From the other side of the peristyle it is possible to reach the bathroom which reproduces on a smaller scale and with refined pictorial decorations a typical thermal complex. The silver plate found in this house testifies to the wealth of the inhabitants.

▶
Portrait of the poet Menander

The House of the Large Fountain

The house of the large-fountain and that of the small fountain derives its name from a special ornament which is found in the garden. From a stone nook covered with vitreous polychrome mosaic work springs a fountain, the water of which gathers in a small basin covered with marble plates. Small bronze statues and marble masks all help to make the effect more lively. It is not easy to recover mosaic wall decorations such as these during archaelogical excavations — much more common are the mosaic floors — this is because these wall decorations are more susceptible to damage and ruin. Thus we sometimes get the wrong impression that the ancients used mosaics only for floor decorations but here Pompeii gives us a valuable idea of wall mosaics.

The Large Fountain - Detail

▶
**The House of the Large Fountain
Nymphaeum in Mosaic**

The House of Venus in the Shell

Here the construction is concentrated around the garden along which there is a two-sided porch. On the end wall is an airy, vivid painting with subjects relating to the garden — hedges with flowery bushes, marble basins with doves and even a Mars. The large composition in the centre of the painting is Venus sailing the sea in a shell and escorted by two Amoretti. Artistically speaking this is a modest work but must be appreciated for its decorative taste which harmonizes pleasantly with the garden and its flora.

The House of the Orchard

The vivid decoration which gives the name to this house (also called "the house of the floral cubicles") adorns the walls of two cubicles, one near the atrium and the other near the tablinum. The paintings show fig-trees, cherry-trees, strawberry trees and lemon-trees which must have been rare in ancient Campania — birds and other animals give life to the picture which undoubtedly was inspired by the fertile Pompeian countryside of that period. In the lower part of the painting trees, basins, enclosures give the idea of a garden and the fact that these subjects have been used for a painting inside the house and not in the garden or porch suggests that the house was inhabited by a rich fruitgrower who chose subjects close to his daily life. From Egyptian subjects found in the same cubicles it is also thought that worship of Dionysus-Osiris was practised here.

The Loreio Tiburtino's House

This is a house of simple, harmonious proportions and a large part is given over to the green of the garden which stretches out at the back of the house and to the long loggia covered by a pergola. A stream with a small waterfall, fountains and statues of muses, animals and hermas adorned the whole setting. At the end of the loggia, in the open air, a triclinium is decorated with mythical subjects Pyramus and Thisbe and Narcissus and even if these paintings have no artistic value they are interesting as they were signed by the artist and man called *Lucius*. The paintings in the hall were painted with more care — on two uninterrupted freizes are depicted the Trojan cycle and the labours of Hercules. In another small room is an elegant painting of many figures one of which is the figure of a priest of Isis and is thought to be the portrait of one of the inhabitants of the house.

◀
The Garden

▶
Porch and Garden

The Giulia Felice's House

This house was built at the east end of the town and its several parts surround a large garden which is bordered on one side by a marble pillared porch and on the other by a pergola whilst in the centre is a large pool. Behind the porch are many rooms one of which is the triclinium and then the thermal quarter which we learn from the inscription was let for public use. Here we can recognise the characteristic elements — *frigidarium*, *tepidarium*, *calidarium* and a *laconicum* for *sudationes*. Nearby is a block used for shops which had an upper storey and finally behind the villa is a large area with a kitchen garden and an orchard.

The Diomede's Villa

This villa opens out onto the Graves Way with a small entrance which leads into the peristyle around which are situated the various parts of the villa. To the east is the thermal quarter with a small porch and a pool for cold baths while to the north and south are a succession of rooms including the triclinium and an apse hall with three large windows. Opposite the entrance is the tablinium which leads on to the other part of the villa formed by a garden in a square area surrounded by porches supporting a balcony while in the centre of the garden is a pool and a summer triclinium. This is a classic example of an urban villa plan in the imperial roman age.

The Peristylium - Detail

The Peristylium

The suburban Villa of Marina Gate

A suburban villa standing near the Marina Gate is sometimes mistakenly called the Imperial Villa. It was built making use of the defensive wall when this no longer had a defensive task and is constructed in terraces so as to appreciate the surrounding panorama. The villa was partially destroyed in 62 AD but still shows evidence today of its complex architectural design. A long porch with paintings of the third style surround the garden and lead to the bedrooms, a triclinium hall and other rooms. The hall, preceded by a vestibule and bordered by passages is one of the largest covered rooms we know in Pompeian buildings and contains fine paintings showing scenes of Theseus and Icarus The villa which has not been completely excavated must have been large and rich with other rooms, porches and a garden of which we only know a part.

So called Imperial Villa - Detail of the Porch

The Villa of Mysteries

This is perhaps the most famous and most highly admired house in Pompeii because it is the finest and most complete example of a large suburban villa and also because of its various rooms decorated with artistically superior paintings especially in the triclinium hall which contains the famous frieze which gives the villa its name. The excavation of this villa which began in 1909-10 is not yet complete but it is thought that the small part still buried can add little to what we already know. The first plan of the villa

Grand Hall - Painting   **Reading of the Ritual and young Girl offering ▶**

goes back to the second century BC but was later enlarged and rebuilt as a luxury house and its golden moment came during the Augustan Age when it became part of the imperial state property. However after the earthquake it was reduced to a rustic villa and its last owners belonged to the Istacidi family. It is a large four-sided building built on a slope so that it rests partially on the ground and partially on a covered porch. The entrance, not completely excavated leads onto a road of which we know only a small part and which was perhaps linked to the Graves Way. To the sides of the entrance are the servants quarters with equipment for making pasta, also an oven, the kitchens, wine pantry and a wine press. From the entrance passing through a small atrium we reach the peristyle where the true nucleus of this house begins with rooms and halls for different uses and a group of thermal rooms. Here is the large atrium, the tablinium and an apse verandah with a view of the sea. To the sides are still more rooms, cubicles, the triclinium with the famous large freize and porches dividing different groups of rooms. Passing through the verandah to visit the villa we note that this part of the buildings has hanging gardens and is supported by the aforementioned covered porch. The painted wall decorations have unequalled interest and reflect the different periods of the building's life and the various uses it was put to. The decorations of the III and IV styles are less interesting but the tablinium is noteworthy with its black walls and Egyptian type symbols — however the most valuable are the paintings of the second style which were spared the changes the villa underwent during the last period. A cubicle with figures linked to the myth and worship of Dionysus is decorated in the same style and this cubicle is used as an anteroom for the triclinium hall. The large freize in this hall is of the second style and is the most complete example of a special type which we seldom see in the paintings of this period — here in fact is a continuous representation which occupies all the walls in the rooms with natural size figures. This freize was perhaps executed towards the middle of the first century BC by a local artist who drew inspiration from the works of Greek painters or was influenced by that style of painting and its classical rules. Scholars cannot agree to the paintings' meaning as it does not deal with an easily identifiable subject — it is composed of different scenes one after the other which deal with different stages of a rite about which we have no information. It is believed that the painting is related to the mistery worship which existed together in the Greek-Roman world with the state religion but which was known only by a few selected men. Many people believe that the freize deals with the various phases of the initiation of a bride to dionysiac mysteries — mysteries which were found in Campania in the Roman age. Thus we see in the various scenes both human and divine figures. The reason why the frieze was painted here can be explained by the fact that the ladyowner was an initiator and minister of this cult. The freize begins on the north wall near a small door — in the first scene a boy is reading the sacred ritual under the guidance of a noble lady while a woman in a mantle listens. The next scene depicts the sacrifice and offering with a pastoral group including Silenus playing the lyre.

▶

The Scourged and the Naked Bacchante

The Villa of Mysteries - The Sacrifice and Silenus playing   The Terrified ▶

The wall at the end of the hall is dominated by two divinities to whom the rites are relative, Dionysus and Arianna, then to one side Silenian satyrs are intent on some mysterious deed whilst on the other side a woman reveals the symbol of fertility whilst a winged figure is in the act of striking with a *flagellum*. On another wall a whipped woman seeks refuge in her friends lap whilst nearby a naked Bacchante dances seized by orgiastic excitement. Lastly the bride dresses and the rite ends showing her sitting and mantled now the initiated and mystic bride of the god.

Mills, Wines and Shops

The shops and workshops in Pompeii offer us a valuable insight into the daily life of the Pompeians and help to clarify what the contemporary writers wrote. Not only daily life with its vivid human aspects but also social and economic life with all its fascinating problems and multiform aspects. The shops and workshops set in rows along the roads of the town occupy the ground floor rooms which have often only been transformed into shops during the last years of Pompeii when the merchants fluorished and the rich families began to decline. Often we can see that a mezzanine wooden floor had been constructed to provide an abode for the seller (we still see this practice in our southern towns) and signs often remain of a small wooden porch which overlooked the road. On the outer wall of the shops we can note painted signs which drew

Mill and Oven

The Baker's Shop ▶

passer-by's attention to what was sold in that particular shop or signs depicting divinities who it was hoped would help and protect the shop. Inside the shops and workshops we can gather from the furniture and equipment as well as from painted or graphite inscriptions what was sold there. At the entrance to the shops a long stone bench covered with marble or painted plaster was used to exhibit the goods — bulging amphoras on the counter held corn, oil and wine and sometimes residues of the contents have been found during the excavations. A product found in the well-sealed amphoras is the *garum*, a kind of fish sauce and we can read the name of the sauce and the manufacturer of the sauce on the amphoras. From all this evidence we can find out the agricultural production of the area, the goods imported and the diet of the Pompeians. We must not forget the many *tabernae*, really public-houses and the *thermopolia* which rather looked like our bars — these were places where people met for a drink and a chat. One of these establish-

A Shop - Detail

ments was managed not by a landlord but by girls who seemed to have been activists during the last Pompeian elections. The bakeries have also proved to be very interesting — we can see the mill stones with which they produced the flour and nearby the table where the dough was kneaded and at the end of the room the oven. Pieces of carbonized bread have been found during the excavations and also an inscription testifying to the goodness of Pompeian bread. Obviously all the most important activities are recognizable in the shops — bread was sold either at the bakery where it was produced or in special bakershops, there were fruiterers one of whom was a certain *Felix*, vegetable sellers, shoemakers, washerwomen and dyers, carpenters and blacksmiths and pastry cooks who, judging from the cake forms found must have been very skillful. To complete the picture we have the brothel giving us an interesting insight into the morals and the *hospitium* a modest inn organization for people who came from a distant place.

A Shop

Aerial view of the excavations

Sepulchral Monuments

The principal roads connecting Pompeii with neighbouring towns were bordered, as was the classic custom, not only by villas and country houses but also by sepulchral areas, the necropolis. Side by side with poor graves are several rich sepulchral monuments which belonged to personages who held an important place in the history or public life of the town as well as to the most influential Pompeian families. Styles vary, some reflect Greek-Hellenistic funeral architecture while others follow the Roman Italic tradition and yet others reflect particular tastes and requirements. Often the points of greater distinction from the artistic point of view are found in the sepulchral enclosure which is surrounded by a low wall and included a small open area for burials in the earth and a columbarium room where the urns for ashes were kept. Two extraurban roads outside Pompeii possess the majority of these monuments, they are Sepulchre or Graves Way leading from the Herculaneum Gate and the Nucerina Way but others have also been found outside Stabia Gate, Vesuvius Gate and places more distant from the town. Along the Sepulchre Way we can see: the *Istacidis* Mausoleum — a circular temple set on a high podium and adorned with statues only one of which survives today, then there is the Tomb of Garlands one of the most ancient with its fine relief decoration, *M. Umbricio Scauro's Sepulchre* showing scenes from gladiator games in his honour, *C. Munazio Fausto* and his wife *Nevoleia Tyche's* sepulchre including a marble altar on which are sculpted a funeral ceremony and a ship lowering the sails — an important example of sculpture of the last years of Pompeii. Here also is the *Family Ceia's* sepulchre adorned with statues. No less interesting are the sepulchres found along the Nucerina Way; the *Cuspis* sepulchre with a columbarium room on top of which stands a circular monument, this same circular monument is found inside the funeral enclosure of the *Veia Barchilla's Sepulchre*. There is the funeral area belonging to the *Flavia family* who were freedmen with aediculas showing their dead's portraits and a square temple sepulchre which has statues of the dead in sitting positions, also the large exedra sepulchre of the priestess *Eumachia*, *M. Ottavio* and his relatives' monument formed by a four colonnaded temple with the dead's statues, the *Stronnis' Sepulchre* like a podium with crouched lions executed in the Hellenistic style and *Vesonis'* aedicula monument again with statues of their dead. All these funeral monuments

▶
The Graves Way and Herculaneum Gate

72

The Graves outside Nocera Gate

usually have inscriptions telling us the names and rank of the personages buried there and in this way we can see the activity they
carried out in Pompeii, follow episodes in their life, identify their
house, the public works they performed and finally the place where
they are buried.

Examples of Sepulchral Architecture

Organic substances were not preserved over the centuries as those objects made from inorganic materials – slowly they disintegrated leaving an empty space – during the excavations when an empty space was noticed plaster casts were made to obtain the shape of what was in the empty space before it disintegrated. In this way casts have been made of the corpses of victims of the eruption, of trees, wooden objects, doors cartwheels furniture etc. Here in the Pompeian antiquarium are kept many of these plaster casts – important relics of what otherwise would have been lost.

Tracing of a Corpse

Tracing of a dog

Tracings of corpses
found in a garden

ARCHAEOLOGICAL MUSEUM

The Naples Archaelogical Museum has perhaps one of the wealthiest and most complete collections of art treasures and documents pertaining to the Classic World. This is partly because many treasures have been supplied from the excavations of the two buried cities Pompeii and Herculaneum and also because the collections of the Farnese Family are now housed in the museum. Furthermore for more than a century when other local museums were not yet in existence any discoveries made in the Kingdom of Naples were automatically sent to the Museum together with various collections (Borgia di Velletri, Lovisato, Spinelli etc.).

The collection of the findings from Pompeii and Herculaneum was begun in the Royal Villa of Portici when the excavations were begun in 1738.

The Farnese collections came to Naples through King Carlo di Borbone the last heir of that family through his mother Elisabetta second wife of Philip V of Spain. The books, paintings and smaller collections were kept in the Palace of Capodimonte (1738 project of Giacomo Antonio Medrano). The ancient sculptures which were in the Farnese villas in Rome were brought to Naples in 1787 and in this year it can be said that the Naples Museum came into being as King Ferdinando decided to give the various collections a permanent exhibition and thus in the following years the "remains" from Portici, the Farnese collections together with those already at Capodimonte were placed in the "palazzo" which is today the Museum.

This building was erected originally in 1585 as a stable but later Viceroy Pedro Fernan dez de Castron Count of Lemos (1610-1616) had the building transformed into a University by Giulio Cesare Fontana. And here Giambattista Vico taught rhetoric.

Halfway through the 17th century the "palazzo" was enlarged by Sanfelice and Fuga and its function changed. In fact as the Gesuits were suppressed in the Kingdom of Naples in 1767, the University was moved to the buildings belonging to the Jesuit Order (1777) and 10 years later the Museum came into being. Through various happenings the Archaelogical Museum (which until 1957 together with the Art Gallery now in Capodimonte formed the Naples National Museum) has continued to increase its collections and up-date their order within the limits imposed by the architecture of the "palazzo".

(from "A. de Franciscis", Guide of the Archaelogical National Museum of Naples, 4th edition, di Mauro Publisher, 1974).

MEDEA

The sorceress Medea contemplates killing her children to avenge her husband Jason who intends marrying another woman. The myth, which inspired both Greek and Roman poets, is depicted in this painting at its most dramatic moment: the figure of Medea which seems torn by various passions is contrasted by the two children who play nearby completely unaware of the fate in store for them, watched over, although in vain, by an old pedagogue.

MOSAIC OF ALEXANDER

This mosaic found in Pompeii, made up the pavement of one of the main rooms in the House of the Faun, one of the oldest and richest houses in Pompei. The last phase of a battle is depicted, probably the Battle of Isse (333 BC), and shows the Greek-Macedonian army of Alexander the Great and the Persian army under Darius. The Persians flee from the charge of the Macedonian army and the two kings clash.

Alexander on horseback victoriously gives chase, whilst Darius flees in his chariot, his followers sacrificing themselves for his safety. Points to note are the sense of multitude although few figures are in fact used and the single but dramatic episodes. The choice of sober colours and light tones result in the sense of unity and compactness of the overall scene.

This Pompeian mosaic is a reproduction of an original by a great artist of the last decades of the 4th century BC.

From written evidence various hypotheses have been developed as to the identity of the original artist including Filosseno of Eretria, Aristide of Thebes or Elena of Alexandria.

MOSAICS OF DIOSKURIDES

In Cicero's villa in Pompeii two mosaic pictures signed by Dioskurides of Samos have been found. One shows a group of strolling musicians and the other a sorceress with her young clients. Both scenes are thought to have been taken from a Greek comedy rather than everyday life. The choice of colours and composition of the groups give in the first a sense of squalor and in the second the idea of women gossiping. The technique is very expert with chiaroscuro, glazing and shading which helps suggest depth and space.
Dioskurides was probably inspired by asiatic paintings of the 3rd century BC and these mosaics are datable about 100 BC.

▶
MARINE FAUNA

Hellenistic art which includes many subjects from nature could not exclude the variable and changing world of marine fauna. From a work, today lost, of an expert artist of the time, are derived some mosaics which differ little one from another and which are not comparable with the original. Here we have the fauna group superimposed on a seascape with rocks. The acute observation of nature enables us to recognize the various species and give a very lifelike quality to this extremely accurate mosaic. The central episode is a battle between an octopus and a lobster which was a popular theme in the narratives of ancient writers.

WALL PAINTING

The Roman murals found in Pompeii and other cities buried by the eruption of Vesuvius show a large variety of subjects as well as quality of expression. Besides the mythological paintings which decorate the centre walls are figures of women, cupids, animals, still lives and decoration of every kind.

▶
PORTRAIT OF A WOMAN IN MOSAIC

An echo of the mosaic art of the Hellenistic period is found in a delicate portrait which was set in the floor of a villa in Pompeii. This is probably the portrait of a poetess or princess of the period and not of the owner as is usually thought.
The young woman is soberly dressed in a tunic and cloak with a simple necklace and gold earrings.

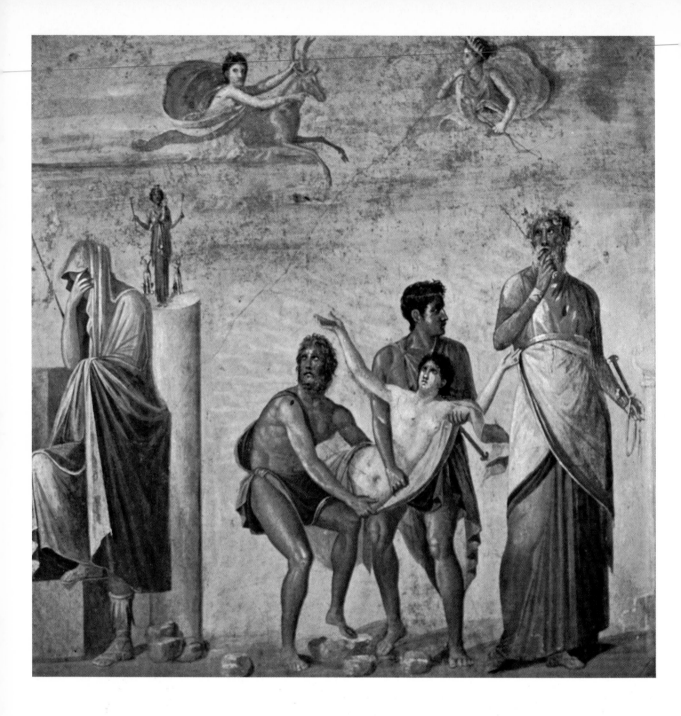

THE SACRIFICE OF IPHIGENIA

Iphigenia is being led to the sacrifice, immolating herself for the propitious departure of the Greek heroes for the Trojan War. The priest Calchas seems rather unwilling to perform his duty and Agamemnon leader of the troops and also father of the victim turns his back on the scene and covers his face with his hands. Above Artemis and a nymph bear the deer which will at the last minute take Iphigenia's place for the sacrifice. The picture is dated in the Roman era and appears to be based on a work by the painter Timante (V-IV century BC), who was famous for the dramatic expressions he gave to the personages he depicted.

PERSEUS AND ANDROMEDA

The hero has killed the sea monster to which Andromeda had been offered as a sacrifice and frees the girl from the rock to which she had been tied. This is the final phase in one of Perseus adventures. This episode is represented many times in paintings in Herculaneum and Pompeii but in differing styles in such a way that another painting of the same subject by the Athenian Nicias (second half of VI century BC) can only be considered an inspiration which Roman artists then interpreted in accordance with their own style and capacity.

PORTRAIT PAINTINGS

Portraits must have been extremely common in the Roman world, it was the custom to keep portraits of ancestors in the houses and in fact many have been found in Pompei, some of which are justly famous.

The most beautiful of this series is a painting depicting, it is thought, Paquio Proculo and his wife.

This is a vivacious portrait of a Pompeian couple of what we would today refer to as the lower middle class. In fact the couple insisted on being depicted holding a papyrus volumen and a wax tabella so as to give an air of importance and seriousness to their portrait – all in vain as they cannot disguise their rather modest background.

Rather more delicate is the portrait of a girl who
seems to be looking for inspiration in the tabella
in her left hand while holding a pen to her lips.

THE RUSTIC CONCERT

Pan and the nymphs tune up for a rustic concert; Pan plays the syrinx and the nymphs a lyre and double tibia. Another nymph is listening. The drawing is sober and the balanced composition reveals a Greek inspiration. However the scene is depicted in a rocky landscape including large trees and a house which is completely Roman inasmuch as the Romans liked to create surroundings for their figures. The landscape with these light tones gives a fairylike setting for the mythical figures which with their colourful clothing are vivacious by comparison.

The painting is in the IIIrd Pompeian style dating from the Augustus era.

EUMACHIA

In Pompeii, the priestess Eumachia had built at her own expense most of the huge building destined to be the seat of the *fullones* and the depository and selling place of wool and woollen clothing. In this building which was sited in the Forum, the *fullones*, as a sign of their gratitude, erected a statue in her honour. The priestess is represented with her head covered by a mantle, the drapery is executed with grace and accuracy, revealing in the classic lines its derivation from a Greek type of statue of the IV century BC.

The influence of Greek art is noted also in the face, here instead of the typical feminine face found in Roman portraits the features are rendered in the style of Praxiteles – the expression is indefinite, the eyes deep and dreamlike. This statue was executed in the Tiberian era.

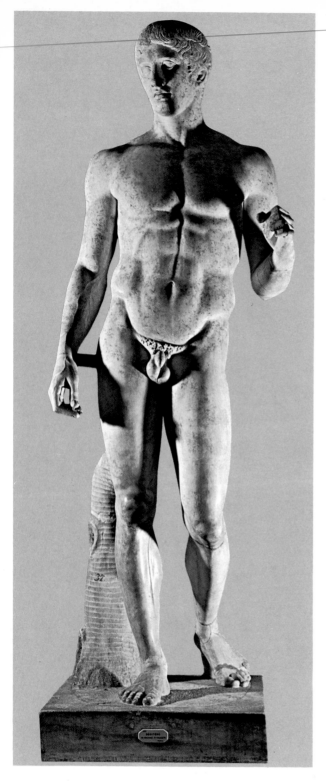

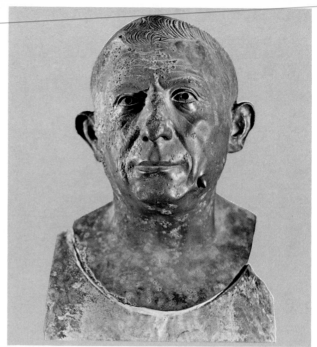

and the best inasmuch as it follows most closely Polycle tus' theories is now in the Naples Museum having been found in the Samnite Gymnasium in Pompeii. The limbs are proportioned in accordance with precise mathematical calculations and are balanced as the weight of the body rests on the right leg and the right arm is at rest whilst the left arm is in action corresponding with the leg behind. The whole figure is perfectly balanced and rests lightly on the ground. The structure of the nude is rendered, although not forcedly so, by the features of the anatomy and the muscles which follow the pose of the figure. Here in synthesis we find th body perfect aspired to in Greek art and the athletic ideal.

L. CECILO

This is one of the most famous portraits of Pompeii. It was found in the house of L. Cecilo Giocondo, a rich Pompeian banker, who lived and was active in the 10 years which preceded the eruption of Vesuvius and it is generally accepted that this portrait is of Cecilo himself.

However the style leads us to believe that it was produced in the Augustan era and it is more probably his father who is represented. Worth noting is the great detail with which the facial features are represented with extreme realism and yet without artifice in such a way that the features are neither accented nor exaggerated.

The validity of this portrait as a work of art is in the vivacity and simpleness with which the sculptor has been able to portray the human features.

POLYCLETUS' SPEARMAN

Polycletus of Argo, the great sculptor who was a contemporary of Phidias, in a theisis called "Kanón" expounded his theories on the ideal form of the human body and the proportions of its various parts. He applied these theories in a statue of a young man with a lance (doriforo). The original work in bronze has been lost but there are many copies of the Roman era

APOLLO THE ZITHER PLAYER

From one of the most beautiful villas of Pompeii (the Villa of the Zither Player) comes a bronze statue of Apollo holding a zither. The anatomy and the ponderousness of the figure is in the severe ancient style and the face has a noble expression. Other examples of this type of statue are known, all from the Roman era, and from their characteristics of style would seem to originate from an original by Phidias executed in his youth when he has not completely developed his artistic personality.

EPHEBE OF VIA DELL'ABBONDANZA

Considered a Roman copy of an attic original of half-way through the V century BC, the Ephebe found in Pompei in a house in Via dell'Abbondanza is in reality a Roman neo-classic work datable in the Augustan era which re-echoes the Greek statues of the classic period. The young figure is shown as a lamp carrier, and supports in his hands two curved hooks from which oil lamps should be suspended.

OLCONIO RUFO

We know that Marco Olconio Rufo was an eminent citizen of Pompeii, he was *duovir* five times, military tribune and priest of Augustus. We have to thank him and his brother Celere for the reconstruction of the theatre and the Pompeians erected two statues in their honour.

Here Olconio is shown in military uniform, above the short tunic he wears a richly decorated armour, while the cloak covers his shoulders and falls over his arms. The sculptor wished to catch the features of this individual with a moderate realistic sentiment necessitated in carrying out an "official" portrait and from the face there is a certain academism which predominated in Rome in portraits of this period. This is therefore an interesting testimony of Pompeian art and the cultural relations between this city and the centre of the Empire. The statue from the style can be dated in the first Augustan era.

NORBANO SORICE

As often happens with portraits found in Pompei there is no doubt as to the identity of the person portrayed as the relative inscription informs us that the portrait is of a certain Caio Norbano Sorice who was an actor. In this sculpture there is a lively sense of structural compactness and the expression of the individual characteristics are skillfully rendered by the position of the head which looks directly ahead. The solid facial features create a varied play of lights and volume. The critical interpretation of this work is controversial. It is sometimes included with other Roman portraits of an Egyptian flavour and sometimes with Roman art of the Republican era. It can however be considered a production, perhaps local, in pure italic tradition datable in the last decades of the 1st century BC, that is to say the first Augustan period. This conclusion is drawn from the stylistic analysis and an inscription which refers to a suburb of Pompeii named after the Emperor Augustus.

THE YOUNG SATYR

A young satyr pours wine from a wineskin making the wine gush into the cup which he holds in his hand. In the attempt to maintain the wine skin the body is balanced on parted legs resulting in a lively attitude which shows the play of muscles. This is datable in the Ist century of the Empire. This is one of the most graceful examples of small sculptures in bronze or marble which decorated the houses and gardens and were sometimes used as fountain ornaments, harmonizing the subject, action, setting and the function for which it was destined.

STATUES OF HOUSEHOLD GODS

The gods (larari) which protected the house and family were kept in small shrines. They were usually bronze statues of simple craftmanship often produced in series. A valid example is the group with the goddess of Fortune sitting on a richly adorned throne with the two Lari, omens of prosperity and abundance, on either side. Craftsmanship of the 1st century of the Empire.

GLADIATOR'S HELMETS

In the excavatins of Pompeii a considerable amount of gladiator's armour has been found which differs from others inasmuch as it is richly decorated with figures. It was certainly not functional for battle purposes and therefore it is thought to have been used for wall decoration. The most interesting pieces are two helmets which bear decoration in high relief. On one helmet the last night of Troy is depicted with the various episodes which characterize that tragic event. On the second helmet the apotheosis of Rome is represented in a series of pictures and symbolic personages.
Workmanship of the 1st century of the Empire.

BRONZE VASES

In the Naples Museum is a vast collection of bronze vases which had many uses in the everyday life of the Romans. The vases according to their use had various forms – large bowls, amphorae, jugs, basins etc, obviously varying in size and shape. Corresponding forms are found in clay vases but it should be noted that the bronze vases were enhanced with decorations making them still more valuable. The handles, feet and bottoms in particular were adorned with figures of masks, ornate fruits etc, of handsome craftsmanship.

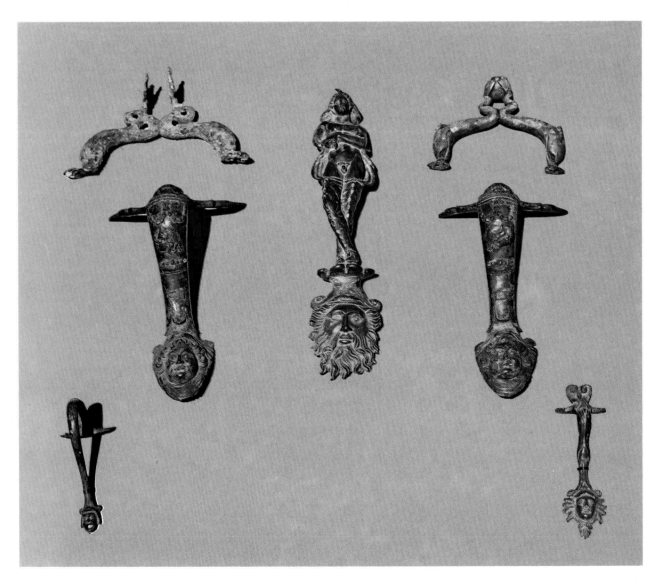

ARTISTIC AND PROFESSIONAL
INSTRUMENTS

Evidence of the various activities of a city's inhabitants can be seen from the tools and instruments brought to light in the excavations. This is in fact the case with Herculaneum and Pompeii.
Here we have musical instruments including sistrum and drums, used in special foreign cult cerimonies such as that of the Isis cult.

Surgical instruments give us an idea of the level medicine and operational techniques had reached in those times and finally there are measuring instruments necessary for land surveying and building so well done by the Romans.

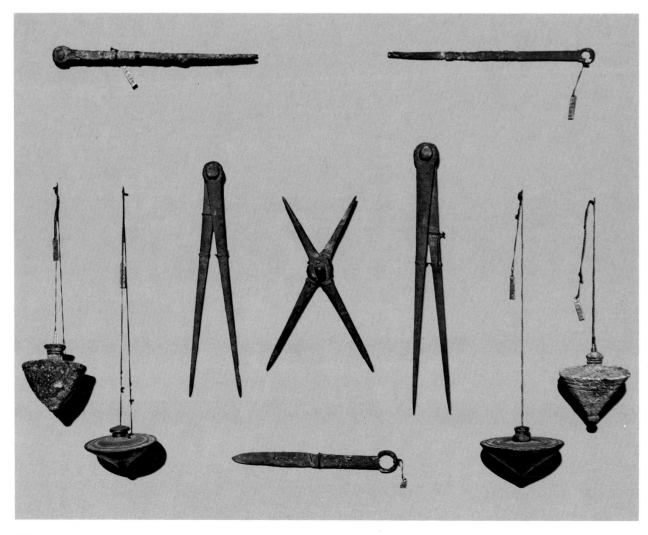

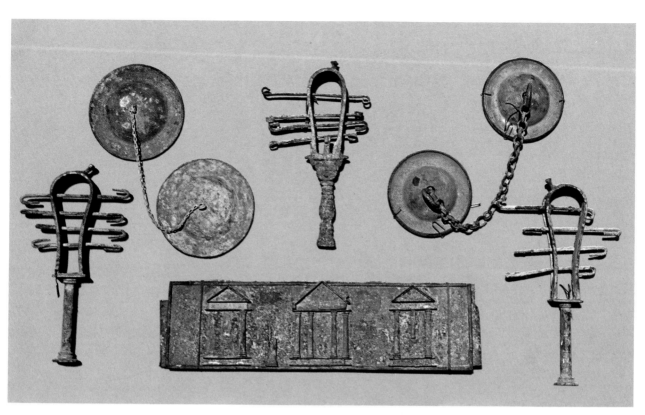

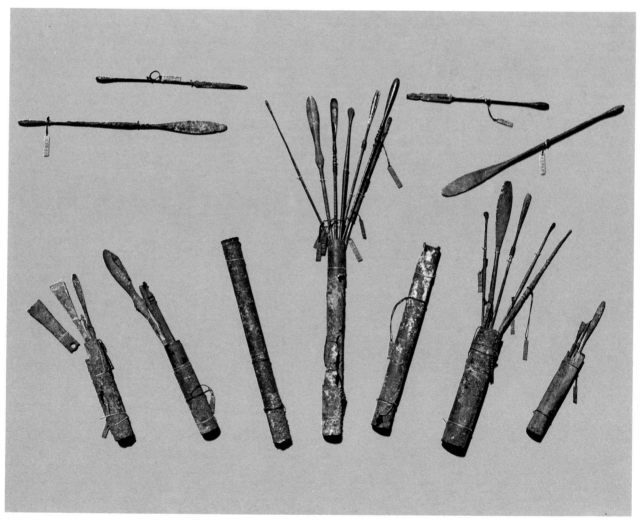

OPLONTIS

Among the towns of southern Campania, which were buried by the Vesuvius eruption in 79 A.D., one is to be found in the ancient written sources, which is named "Oplontis", in the famous cartographic document of the Roman Empire known as "Tabula Peutingeriana", whereas it is named "Omplontis" by the geographer Guidone and "Emplontis-Opolontis" by the Anonymous of Ravenna.

Apart from these references, this centre is not mentioned by any author and in any epigraphic document. Therefore the word was even considered not to be a town name, but a geographers' comment (meaning: destroyed town). The original meaning of the name was looked for phantastically, too, until...... Alessio determined its connection with the name of a tree which is usually to be found in vineyards (Latin word: opulus), the origin of which dates back to the most ancient stratum of our civilisation, the "Mediterranean" one. On the one hand this may be a sign of frequenting continuity, on the other hand it may be an indication that vine-growing had been known since remote ages in the Oplontis area.

From time to time, archaelogical remains have been discovered in the area of modern Torre Annunziata. However it happened by accident or as a result of limited researches, beginning from the first digs in Bourbon times. In this regard, it is to be remarked that some confusion occurred at first: in fact, some documents indicate digs at Pompeii, whereas they should be intended at Torre Annunziata. On the other hand, according to the "Tabula Peutingeriana", Oplontis is situated six miles from Herculaneum and three miles from Pompeii; therefore the real location of ancient Oplontis is undoubtedly in this place. When analyzing the results of the archaelogical discoveries in this area, we note that there were only villas, or better: villas in a certain style and of high artistic level. The only exception could be seen in the ruins of the so-called "Terme Nunziante", which are considered to be the ruins of a thermal building. This should be however better ascertained on the base of our knowledge of the ancient building technique, which is more precise nowadays than at the discovery time. As a matter of fact, there is no trace of streets, shops or other structures – such as public buildings – which are usually typical of towns or villages having their own organization.

Furthermore, when drawing a map of all these ruins, the resulting lining-up runs approximately from East to West, and our villa is no exception.

Therefore we can by right consider Oplontis not as a town-centre with its own town-structure, but rather as a residential centre with big villas situated along the coast-road leading from Neapolis to Herculaneum and Oplontis and from here on forking towards Stabiae, on one side, and towards Pompeii, on the other side.

Our interpretation of the archaelogical data is also supported by the symbol of Oplontis in the "Tabula Peutingeriana", which is sometimes intended as an indication for a thermal building but resembles – in fact – the plan of a villa or villa-hospitium.

Oplontis situation is therefore similar to Stabiae's situation in Roman age, but we cannot say whether Oplontis – like Stabiae – "abiit in villas" at a certain moment of its history, or whether its topographic events were different.

Oplontis is however one of the many places situated all along Naples Gulf from Stabiae to Capo Miseno, i. e. a suitable site for villas belonging to the richest and most famous families from Rome and Campania. Furthermore, we may presume that Oplontis was strictly connected with Pompeii, being perhaps a residential quarter of it.

Among all buildings, which have been mentioned or discovered at Oplontis so far, we are going just to examine Poppea's villa, which has been dug out during the first regular excavation carried out in the area of ancient Oplontis. This excavation was started by us in 1964 and is still in progress.

It has already brought results, which are remarkable from several points of view. It has aroused a great deal of interest in the archaelogical circles and among those who are interested in classic antiquity.

This villa is situated in an area which was already ransacked in Bourbon times, with the usual methods of those times: it is the so-called "Mascatelle" property, where ancient ruins were first found out in 1833. There are documents of dig-trials carried out in 1839 and 1840, on behalf of the Government; these

Cubiculum

works were committed to the assistant-keeper of the Royal Museum, Don Michele Rusca.

According to the scarce documentation of that time, some ruins found out on that occasion could be parts of our villa.

Moreover, it has been ascertained during the recent excavation that those same dig-trials "touched" the villa which is now being taken into consideration. As works progressed, we came across the typical underground-passages, through which they used to explore the subsoil at that time. In one of these passages, which runs along the eastern side of the villa, we could read the following inscription written with charcoal on the white plastered wall and unfortunately soon faded: "Rufolo Antonio, April 9, 1839". Maybe it was the name of a digger or of a visitor of that time. Furthermore we noted that some pieces of the wall-decoration had come unstuck.

In more recent times, Amedeo Maiuri was much interested in this area and bought it for the State, but he had no chance to start exploring.

Through the digging of the villa it was possible to ascertain and precise the stratigraphy of the burying caused by the Vesuvius eruption in the year 79. Slightly sloping from North to South there are, starting from the bottom, four lapillus layers alternating with three ash layers to a total average height of 1,80

Small inner garden with decorations

m. A layer of hardened mud lies above up to an average height of 5 m, on top of which a layer of humus of 1,50 m approximately formed in the course of the centuries. As it was remaked on the occasion of previous explorations in the area of Oplontis, mud burying, which is typical in the area of Herculaneum, lies here above ash and lapillus burying, which is typical in the area of Pompeii. The Vesuvius eruption covered therefore the ground-floor, as well as a part of the upper floor.

As far as we know, the whole consists of the real building and of a large open area stretching out behind it, called viridarium.

As it had originally been planned, the villa should have been largely dimensioned with wide rooms along the central axis and two separated sectors to the West and to the East.

Later on it was remarkably enlarged to the East. To sum up, a number of rooms were located along the central axis of the original building, in South-North direction. They were strictly connected to one another in the planimetric sense and concerning the depth, with the consequent perspective effect.

Regarding its plan and architecture, the style of the villa is particular for its wall-decorations and sculptures.

Interior of the villa: The Altar Room

According to some epigraphic documents and to various finds taken into consideration, Poppea Sabina, the wife of Emperor Nero, lived there for some time. It was presumably a property of the Poppea family, a member of which was the Empress herself. It was one of the richest and most authoritative families in the nearby town Pompeii.

When Campania was ravaged by the earthquake in the year 62 A.D., Poppea's villa was perhaps one of those which, as Seneca wrote (*Nat. Quest.* VI, 1, 2) "sine iniura tremuere" (trembled without being damaged) in the general destruction.

The few damages were patched up easily. No static unbalance and no big troubles due to the earthquake have been observed so far. In other words, there is not the same frame as it is to be often and clearly seen at Pompeii.

Furthermore, various points of the walls were painted again with crude square-stripe-decorations, which represent somehow a banal restoration of the 1st-style decorative system. Poppea may have been living in the villa already at that moment and she lived there until her death. This happened in 65 A.D., when the conditions of the villa were possibly the same as at the moment of the Vesuvian eruption, i. e. uninhabited or occupied only by few domestic servants. As a matter of fact, in the rooms brought to light so far there are no household-

Glass-vase with Pomegranates ▶

Architectural front

furnishings, objects, works of art, which were signs of a suddenly interrupted life in the Vesuvian towns; there is no crockery and no trace of activity in the large kitchen.

On the contrary, everything which was discovered out of order indicates some works in progress: marble columns were lying on the ground along the walls of the large hall, decorative sculptures were piled up in a corner of the arcade, groups of oil-lamps had been wrapped up and put in a corner of a room, as if they had been stored.

Then the Vesuvian eruption occured in the year 79 and it buried everything with a thick layer, as we already said. Due to all these aspects, the villa of Oplontis is one of the most important evidences of that construction type, which had its own particular significance in the Roman world, both with regard to the artistic production and to the socio-economic way of living of this interesting age of our history.

Calidarium

Eastern wall of the hall

Inner garden

HERCULANEUM

A tradition still alive in the Roman age told of the foundation of Herculaneum in relation to the myth of Hercules but in reality the historical development of Herculaneum was not very different from that of the nearby Pompeii and it also was buried by the Vesuvian eruption in 79 AD. However Herculaneum unlike Pompeii was buried by a muddy torrent which then solidified — the wall structures were therefore more damaged but on the other hand the original materials were better preserved especially the wood and for this reason the excavations of Herculaneum have a special interest.

The exploration of the town began in 1738 and was the first systematic excavation ever made of an ancient town even though they worked for many years making use of wells and tunnels through

Aerial view of Excavations in Herculaneum

114

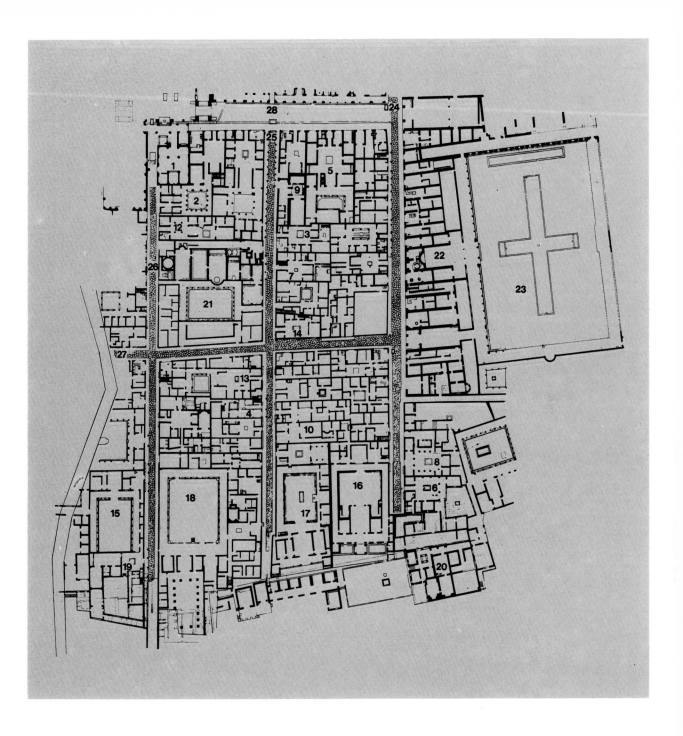

HERCULANEUM
Map of the digs

1 Aedes Augustalium
2 House of the Tuscan Colonnade
3 House of Neptune and Anfitrite
4 Hurdle-house
5 House of the Bicentenary
6 House of the Gem
7 House of the Furniture
8 House of Telefo's Relief
9 House of the Beautiful Yard
10 House of the Alcove
11 House of the Great Portal
12 House of the Two Halls
13 House of the Wooden Dividing Wall
14 Samnite House

15 Argo's House
16 House of the Deer
17 House of the Mosaic Hall
18 Shelter-house
19 Aristide's House
20 Suburbs Baths
21 Central Baths
22 Apsidal Room in the Palaestra
23 Open Area in the Palaestra
24 Fifth Hinge
25 Fourth Hinge
26 Third Hinge
27 Lower Decuman Gate
28 Central Decuman Gate and Forum Area

which they recovered paintings, sculptures, inscriptions and other objects. It was only later that the excavations were made in the open with more scientific methods and of course better results. We only know the approximate layout of the town — it stretched according to a regular plan with right-angled roads and rectangular blocks of one or more houses. In the last period the town was developed somewhat; on the southern walls rich panoramic houses were built, outside the walls a sacred area was formed, also a large thermal building and perhaps other complexes which have still to come to light. The surrounding countryside probably contained villas of which we know only one, the Villa of the Papyri or Pisoni, where a library of papyraceous texts and a collection of sculptures were found. The centre of the town is made up of the maximum decuman where the public buildings, the large gymnasium, the Magistrates seat, a partially explored sacred building and probably the Basilica have been found. The theatre however stands in the northwest part of the town. Private buildings have greater variety and often differ from the usual type we see in Pompeii. Here we have the rare example of a poor house divided into small flats with a central courtyard (Trellis House), there are also interesting examples of atrium houses of Italic type going back to the pre-Roman age. The large house-villas at the edge of the town — the House of Argo, the House of the Hotel and the House of the Mosaic Atrium as well as the House of the Stags all have a special plan.

Card Street

The Fountain of Neptune

Decumanus Maximus

117

The House of Neptune and Anfitrite

The House of the Black Hall

The House of the Mosaic Hall

The House of Telefo's Relief

In these houses the traditional plan is changed, the various rooms don't have the axis disposition and the atrium is turned to the East to West where the entrance is while the peristyles and gardens and attics are turned to the South in a panoramic position with a view of the sea. Many of the shops are well preserved and reveal interesting details of daily life. On the whole Herculaneum was a smaller centre than Pompeii and inhabited in the main by humbler folk, it had no important economic or commercial developments but houses of a more refined sort have been discovered and examples of art confirm this.

The House of the Beautiful Yard

Satyr with wineskin

Drunken Hercules

The House of the Burnt Furniture

The House of the Deer · A Deer assailed by Dogs

A shop - Exterior

A shop - Interior

Apoditerium Baths

The Palaestra

STABIAE

The area where the Roman centre of Stabiae was later to be establish ed was inhabited by Italic people from the VIII century BC as we can see from the necropolis now coming to light. We believe that there were one or more settlements kindred to those in the Sarno Valley and to Nuceria which had its sea outlet here. We do not yet know the position of the fortified centre (the oppidum) of the Samnite period which was later destroyed by Sulla in 89 BC during the civil wars, The town was never rebuilt and the Roman Stabiae was formed by large, rich villas scattered here and there and especially on the slope of the Varano Hill which became one of the most luxurious residential areas for rich Roman families (we have interesting records of this from the ancient writers) owing to the pleasant climate, wonderful panorama of the Gulf of Naples and healthful thermal springs. The archaeological excavations first began during the Bourbonic period, but, as was the custom at the time, recovered again; in the last decades new excavations have been made bringing to light many villas which are among the finest of ancient times. The villas have their residential area along the hillside facing the sea with the servants quarter at the back facing the mountain. Their planimetric design fits with the ground formation and the most favourable orientation so that we have varied and articulate constructions often with more than one level and very similar to the pictures of the villas we see in the landscape paintings found here and in other Vesuvian towns. Paved roads and steps connected the various villas with the nearby shore and the principal main roads of the area. Gardens and peristyles had an important function in the villas and the architects took great care to make them wider and richer with pools, fountains and trees everywhere. There are also very large private thermal installations as in the Villa of S. Marco and also wide reception rooms as in the Villa of Varano. The artistic quality of these buildings is very good not only from the architectural point of view but also for the wall murals and plasters dating back to the first century AD which are often superior to the same Pompeian decorations and also for the furniture recovered here, of which it is sufficient to mention the obsidian cups with gold polychrome scenes and the small stone pieces of Egyptian theme.

ALFONSO DE FRANCISCIS
SUPERINTENDENT OF ANTIQUITIES IN NAPLES

The « Spring »
from Stabiae